Windcalls

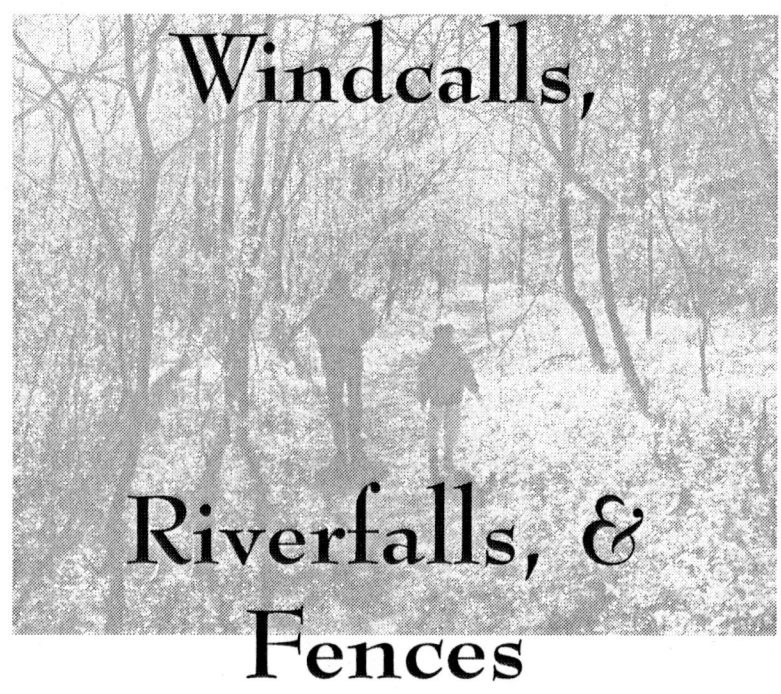

Tamara A. Rutherford

PublishAmerica
Baltimore

© 2006 by Tamara A. Rutherford.
All rights reserved. No part of this book may be reproduced, stored in a retrieval system or transmitted in any form or by any means without the prior written permission of the publishers, except by a reviewer who may quote brief passages in a review to be printed in a newspaper, magazine or journal.

First printing

At the specific preference of the author, PublishAmerica allowed this work to remain exactly as the author intended, verbatim, without editorial input.

ISBN: 1-4241-2201-5
PUBLISHED BY PUBLISHAMERICA, LLLP
www.publishamerica.com
Baltimore

Printed in the United States of America

God has given me so much; my life, my home, my friends, my family, and my son. It is difficult to know to whom this book should be dedicated. So, I dedicate it to Him, who can make all things possible.

"All things work together, for good to those who love God."
Romans 8:28

Windcalls, Riverfalls, & Fences

Windcalls 5
Riverfalls 29
Fences 49
Lost and Found 75

Windcalls

Snowfalls
As Windcalls echo themselves
Whistling a search for beauty
Around barren trees
Drifting seas
Of white
Froze the winter in
So I ponder
Where flowers begin
In spring.

Weather Report

The trees are dressed for winter
In shades of gray and brown
Old scattered clothing set like fire
Upon the misty ground.

Late autumn ushers in the snow
Across the sleeping plain
The earth will rest until she feels
The touch of gentle rain.

It seems the change of seasons
Always takes me by surprise
The bitter winter blowing
And then tulips on the rise.
It must be God's voice speaking
To show us of our place
Life's seasons always changing
Entwined with steadfast grace.

Frost upon my windowpane
Lace patterns like a flower
Quilts piled high and you beside
Me to warm the hour.

The days are short
The nights are long
All the lamps are lit,
The trees are dressed for winter
And I do not mind one bit.

Old Joe's

I never thought I'd say it, but I miss that place.

The old white farmhouse built on a hill was worn beyond its years. Surrounded by giant oak and cherry trees, the roof sagged, the porch creaked, and a gooseberry vine stubbornly clung to the leaning white picket fence, wobbling in the strong prairie wind. Breezes blew my lace curtains to and fro, even though the paned windows were closed. Years ago, someone had dug a root cellar under a trap door off the kitchen, and still setting on a rise of dirt, stood some garden preserves from a previous tenant, as cobwebs hung from the wooden floor beams above my head. The ceilings, walls, and floors of the old home were so sloped, you could roll a ball from one end of the living room to the other by simply setting it down and letting go, and we didn't even consider using the upstairs, it wasn't at all stable. The floor swayed and bounced underneath your feet with every step you took, and a single oil-burning heater, waiting for its glut of fuel in winter, graced the central living room.

But outside the back kitchen door, down a worn cement path, stood a rusted working hand pump over a well, and a 3-seater outhouse was hidden at the edge of the yard. They stood fast as a testimony for past days and ways. Cattle grazed peacefully on sweet alfalfa in the nearby pasture, and quiet filled the air, permeated only by an occasional bird song. The back screen door squeaked and slammed in the wind, as if it was announcing its usefulness amid the ruins.

It was there, on those 5 acres, I dug my first garden—with a spade, and learned about the rich Illinois soil. It was there I made my first from-scratch cherry pie, which took hours and hours of labor. It was there I learned cows have different personalities from each other, and you don't attempt friendship with a bull. And it was there I let go of my city roots and planted my feet in something new.

I decorated my old house with handmade curtains and lace; hung English rose teacups within the attached china cupboard, painted the walls, and arranged the rugs. A drop leaf oak table flanked by two antique library chairs sat near a window, where we ate all our meals, as sunlight filtered through hand blown glass panes, slightly blue-tinted with time. I simmered soup on the stove, tasted my first homegrown tomato, and learned to tell the weather by watching the sky, not the TV. I learned about tornadoes, dust storms, snowdrifts, and the sweet fragrance of daffodils in early spring.

I wove my hopes and dreams among the old walls, gooseberry vines, and pots of steaming tea, claw foot parlor tables, and promises of what was to be. Promises, which like dreams, do not always come true, as I finally realized, at 42.

Looking back, I feel nostalgia for that place. Nostalgia for the angle of the sun that warmed the peeling painted porch, and the smell of the house which was like home cooking, fresh mown hay, and old house musty all in one. But perhaps what I miss the most were the beginnings. The first blazing autumn, the first spring, the first breath of country air, and the first hope I had held in my heart for a long, long time.

Or maybe what I miss is just being 24, and not knowing any different.

Fiancé

For the past three years, he wanted to marry me. I was his only love; the center of his universe, and the tenderness he showed me would melt my heart. Now he wants to marry Sarah, who is nine years old. He says he wants a different wife.

I said that was okay. But at seven years old, a significant part of my son's childhood is over. I am no longer the only woman in his life. Our conversations have become interactive and inquisitive. He displays a sense of humor, but for the most part, remains a basically serious kind of guy when dealing with others.

Still, his childlike world and perceptions are there. He plays imagination games with himself, creating stories and acting out situations. I can hear him upstairs in his room, making sounds of spaceships flying through the stars, with the bad guy eventually losing to the hero. Life still holds some magic.

A good day is when nobody fights; you can find everything you are looking for, and all your creations, Lego, or art projects, come out perfect. Maybe you get the dinner you want, or you get to stay up past bedtime just a few minutes more. You can chase a thousand fireflies in a twilight sea of green, and sunsets are beautiful wonderments, glowing purple, pink and orange on the horizon. Clouds are for pretending you see shapes and creatures, and God and Jesus are number one persons in your life along with Mom and Dad. There are no worries about your food, clothing, or shelter. You bask unknowingly in security of a family and predictable life.

I will miss his days of wanting to marry me. He found shelter on my lap and in my arms. It was the best place in the world, for both of us.

Now, the world is looking bigger, and he no longer wants to marry me. I just pray he will always love me.

The Wardrobe

Trees
Changing coats
Dripping with fire
Fragrance floating upon the breeze
Of an autumn day
Blowing away
To cover my flower garden
For the winter.

Beach Report

It is a smoggy-hazy morning at the beach. Perhaps it is a blessing, as it helps disguise the houses along the distant mountainous shore, creating an illusion of a less populated place. The surfers still go out before sunrise, and return from their rides, surfboards tucked under their arms, appearing as walking seals in slick, black wetsuits. Sunlight dapples the pink sand in long shadows, which reach towards the waves, and people mull about on the Hermosa strand with their cappuccinos, stepping away from the path of bicyclers and joggers. It never ceases to amaze me, the rhythm of people's lives amid the rhythm of the ocean shore...It is a piece of continuity within the chaos of our days.

Dreams

Warm
Softly rain trickled down
As we passed breakfast for love
Aloof
Outside
The gold leaves drifted down
Stubbornly gluing themselves to my patio.
Bedroom windows made for light
I use them
Envisioning my world
Since you sleep
Warm
And softly rain trickled down
As I salted my eggs.
Dreaming.

Weather Watcher

I don't have to look at the calendar.

They know.

The geese are restless in the sky. It is only mid-August, but they are moving; practicing their mid air maneuvers, circling, honking, soaring into the air, and flying between the lakes on a daily basis.

They are not going south, yet. That will come in a few short weeks. It doesn't matter to them September has not arrived yet. As soon as there is a cool snap of weather, they start their mini flights.

My father in law told me if you hear the locusts sing, it would be 6 weeks 'fore frost. According to that, when I first heard them, I figured frost to arrive in early September, which is hard to imagine in the sweltering mid July heat. It was incredibly oppressive this year. But now, the weather has turned cool, and the geese tell me he was right.

It will be soon, very soon.

And the crickets have moved indoors, or tried to. This starts the annual cricket wars in my household. They make noise, and I stake them out with a fly swatter. I have one for almost every room in the house.

Watching the change of seasons can teach us about many things. Life will change. Period. There are always signs ahead of time, so it doesn't catch us by surprise. Some are obvious. A swollen belly and labor pains tell us of the miraculous arrival of a child. Others are more subtle, and easy for us to ignore. Changes in our workplace sometimes signal a time to move on. Changes in our relationships often tell us we again need to adjust ourselves, our way of approaching each other, our level of tolerance and love. To everything there is a season, but sometimes, we cannot figure it out.

But the geese know. They are never wrong, and don't ignore the obvious. They listen to the earth, and somehow, since God has a hand in everything, listen to Him.

As I get older, my physical hearing is becoming duller, drowning out the world. But my mental and spiritual ears are keenly tuning in, and I hope someday, to be like the geese.

I will never miss the signals, the indications of the future, and His directional influence that now guides my life.

This is great.

Cupid

It's not your gentle smile
Or warm embrace
Or your love shining
Through your strengths, hopes, and fears
I need you
And that's what scares me most.
For in this love and need
Lay my heart
My weakest point
Open to your arrow.
So here I am
Playing Russian roulette
And wondering…

Marriage

It wouldn't be right when writing this book to not include something about my husband.

After 17 years, he knows me quite well, all my flaws, my strengths. And now I am beginning to think he can read my mind. But he loves me anyway.

We met at Beach Bum Burt's. It was a picturesque restaurant/lounge in the Redondo Beach harbor. He looked crabby and I did not want to talk to him. I did anyway. The rest is history.

Marriage is not for sissies. It is a work in progress and a test of patience. I have learned that love can be more of an exercise than a romantic feeling. You exercise long enough, and eventually both of you are rowing in the same direction. This takes time. You earn it. It does not come from a book, a self-help site on the web, or by magic. It takes two people bound and determined to keep rowing, no matter what. The rapids and waterfalls come. You keep rowing. The storms roll in. You keep rowing. Someone gets bored. You keep rowing. You are tired, mad, hurt, or just plain worn out. You keep rowing. Eventually you get to the shore, and hopefully, the good stuff.

Like I said, I think he can read my mind. Even better, he cares about what I feel, not just what suits today. He is sensitive to my feelings, and even if I do something stupid, tries to tell me gently. He knows I have a soft spot that can be smashed. But he doesn't.

I don't know what else is in the future for us. Life is always changing. But as long as we are here on earth, we will keep rowing. I can depend on it.

Dirt

It was the funniest thing really. My new relatives thought I was crazy. This was clean dirt, I said. They looked at me like I had lost my mind. I had moved to the country. This was clean dirt.

In a big city, dirt is not what you grow things in. It is what has accumulated on the streets, in the air, from millions of other people. It is also the little patch of ground you are entitled to temporarily own and dig in, which needs so much fertilizer because there is no other life in, or around it. Except of course, that annoying neighborhood dog or wandering cat that thinks it is the best bathroom in the world, twice a day.

The first time I planted a garden, I could not believe you did not have to water it. It will rain, I was told. They were right. I could not believe you did not have to fertilize it with the latest and greatest brand of grow granules. The earth here is dark brown, like velvet almost. It holds the moisture, and has many nutrients. It brings forth life and an abundance of food in a relatively short growing season. It is amazing.

When I was young, my mother was an avid gardener of Midwest roots. Wherever we lived, the yard was always beautiful. I thought she was a fanatic. She told me that everyone should garden, and you can learn so much from it. I thought she was talking about the scientific aspects, not the other, hidden lessons. She was right.

I have learned, from the dirt, where I come from. Without it, I would not survive. I need it to grow my food. The earth does not depend on the latest computer chip to survive, the stock market, or mankind's desire for bigger and better things. It just needs to be lovingly tended, and in return, gives us what we need for life. I am beginning to think that the Native Americans were on the right track. Life may not have been too fancy, but it was satisfying. It was all tied into the earth. Food, shelter, clothing, it all comes from here.

This is a fact that is all too easy to ignore when living in the city. Food comes from the grocery store, clean and neatly packaged. Likewise, clothing. Shelter comes from the building supply store. Things like this are taken for granted, because someone else got their hands dirty doing it. Someone else dealt with the basic things in life, so others did not have to. And the pay wasn't even too good.

The Midwest farmers persevere because the earth has its own reward. You cannot put a price on a sunset over an open field, or the smell of a fall harvest in the air. You cannot put a price on the picturesque scene of a tractor on the horizon, or a million golden bushel of grain going into the grain elevator. The fragrance is wonderful, the reward of satisfaction immeasurable, and connection with the earth goes full cycle.

Somewhere there is a person shopping in a store, complaining about the dirt on the vegetables. As for me, I will enjoy a sunset tinted orange by crop dust, and wash my veggies off.

My Garden

My garden is one of memories
While it sleeps in the winter I dream
Only to be awakened with rains
Of the Midwest spring.

Iris from my grandmother
Oregano from a friend
Flowers with seeds I'll gather
At the season's end.

Fragrant and sweet emerging
Boisterous summer's display
Crisp bright beauty in autumn
To recall on a colder day.

I remember a smile so knowing
And laughter once shared with mirth
The cycle of life ever circling
Season's death
And then
Rebirth.

Coffee

When young, I often wondered what the attraction was for older people to just sit around, drink coffee at the local diner, and talk. Just a bunch of old wrinkled faces setting over steaming cups of Java, solving the world's problems, and reminiscing about the old days. Where was the joy and purpose in that?

I now realize it is simple. It is because they can.

They have the luxury of time and can go to the coffee shops cause they did exactly what I am doing now, working hard, saving money, raising a family, and being involved in others lives, communities, and churches. Just the thought of sitting with a bunch of friends on a daily basis conversing is an indulgence at this point in my life.

Really, I do not mind. I enjoy the opportunity to raise a family, work, and watch the sunrise in the morning. After all, what are the alternatives? Outside fantasy, there are none. I would not give up my family for all the lotto tickets in the world.

The real joy in life is in the doing, in the every day, in the looking back at a job well done. It is in the satisfaction knowing you did what was right for your family and God, not yourself. It is being able to kiss your child goodnight, and look at them square in the face, honestly. Being warm. Being safe. Being fed.

Really, the world is black and white. The gray areas are just political spinning. You either do or you don't. Everything in between are just excuses and lies to convince you otherwise.

Don't be fooled, especially by yourself. Life is short. I will have wrinkles because I have earned them one day at a time, and memories given to me by the grace of God. I plan on looking back, and reminiscing over a cup of coffee.

Because I can.

Riverfalls

Riverfalls

Singing waters
Laughing sky
Native prayers
Swiftly rise.

Moon washed mesa
Northern lights
Native honor
Is held high.

Wind blows brushing
Grass and corn
The People's spirit
Is reborn.

Tatonka graze
Where once they roamed
Sitting Bull
Has come back home.

Judgment

Nature will prevail
When time is left
To work its own purpose
Which leads all
Back to the Creator's hand
And
Your work is worth
What your motives were
Within your actions.

Poem

Funny
Frozen puddles
Crystaled edge surrounds
Rink for little Elves
To take Fairies dancing.
Frosty.

Toby

All life is spirit
Like wind through the trees
The leaves touch each other
In the dancing breeze
Leaves will die come a winter's day
While somewhere
The wind
Has gone out to play.

Tribute to Hannah

All that is left of her homestead is a stand of tall trees and clumps of flowers overgrown with prairie grass.

The first time I saw her, the old woman was sweeping dirt off the edge of an elevated front porch on to the lawn. She was hunched and wrinkled like an old dried apple, wearing a faded red print apron and not-so-dainty leather work boots beneath her housedress, which came from a five-and-dime store, long ago closed for business. I heard she was a widow, and the clothes she wore; combined with the large straw hat on her head told me she was a sensible, frugal woman. Sometimes, I would see her just sitting on a dining room chair, brought out to the wooden porch that faced the road, enjoying the sway of trees above her and singing birds of the day.

It did not matter to Hannah that her family farmhouse occupied land now bordering the north edge of a rapidly growing town. Quaint but small, the single story house was painted white with green trim, bore old gray asbestos roof shingles, and must have had no more than five rooms. Original windows still graced the simple structure designed around the turn of the 20th century, and sometimes on a sunny day, she would have them all flung open for housecleaning, white curtains flapping over the sashes and waving in the wind. Every spring, she would tie a scarf over her hair; and hanging on the laundry line would be small rugs, which she furiously beat out dust from over and over again. There were seemingly little luxuries and no fireplace, only a heating vent for an oil stove that stood above the roofline. Yellow and orange daylilies grew amid the tall broom grass near the edge of the homestead, and the fields that surrounded it were farmed as the rhythm of her life pulsed, season in, season out.

It was not even two weeks after she died, the weeds began to take over, and her family sold the farm where she was born to a local developer. One day, as I drove by, the tiny house was gone. It looked like it simply vanished, without a trace except for the empty spot where it once stood, along with a few remaining daylilies, clinging to a memory of someone who used to tend them. The homestead remained that way for two years, until the development permits were received.

Then, the heavy equipment came: the bulldozers, the earthmovers, the hi-hoes, the backhoes, dump trucks, and road graders. Now, a retention lake is being dug in the field north of where her home stood with water canals feeding into it. The earth, which was once was a rich dark brown has turned to orange clay as the machinery digs into the land preparing for a subdivision of expensive homes she could have never imagined while living her simple, uncomplicated life in the old farmhouse.

I drive by there now, the trees still tall and swaying, but bulldozers and metal skids are parked where the home once stood, and the daylilies have been crushed. Still, I can envision Hannah on her porch, holding high and tipping a basket full of wheat into a metal wash bin, separating grain as the wind carried chaff away into the horizon, the trees dancing above her in harmony with the rhythm of her life, and the birds echoing their songs to greet her.

It is how she would have wanted me to remember her.

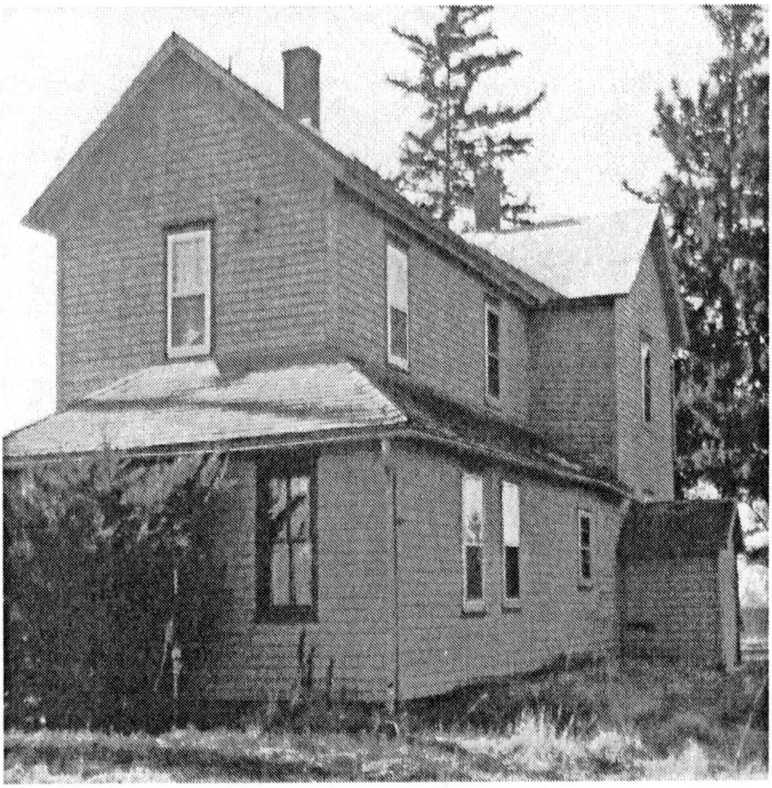

House

She is ancient
Outdated
Old clothing out of style
No one wants her anymore
She is but a skeleton
With just a door
And empty windows gazing
Out on what once was
The hope for her future.

Milena

Paint me a picture
With your words once again
Of sun swept beaches
And sandtoes wiggling
And castles surrendering to the sea.
Think of me
The gulls cry
Far away
Only in my mind
And once again time
Exists there
For us to share
The moment's joy.

Reflections

I look into the mirror
And do not see my face
But that of my mother
Gazing back at me
As if 30 years ago.

I look upon my mother
And find
My grandmother of yesteryear
Her smile and laugh the same.

My grandmother must look at me
And envision
Herself so long ago
A younger woman
Not quite so tired and worn.

I see my child
And remember the feeling of being five
Having kisses that heal everything
And love
That knew no bounds.

Truly this is a gift
To be able to look
Into a past I'll never know
And a future I will become
And wonder
Of what I may never see.

For Matt

My love for you
Has always reached
Before your beginning
And beyond our parting
And exists today
For you
As it always will
Whether I'm here
Or there
You can close your eyes
And see my soul
Feel my hand
And know
You will always be
My beloved child.

Snowflakes

A dream
White magic falling
Silent touching thoughts
Drift downward towards sleeping trees.
Soft.

Old Photographs

Light reflecting on air
Like ghosts rising above
The prairie set on fire
By the Sun
Old houses once
Stood in the wind as fortresses
And havens
Amid the spirit of adventure long gone
And fallen
To the soil and blown
Upon the breeze.
Now left as only reflections
And memories
And old photographs
Yellowed with time.

Spectacles

Your selfishness
Blinds your love
Tugging you along
This road called life
And you wonder why you are not happy
So selfishness says 'it's me, not satisfied'
As love sits alone
Crying in the dark.

Dandelion

Lion Flower
Specks of gold
On the hillside
Glories unfold
Only later
To be pale and gray
And with fairy wishes
Driftdance away.

Artist

Sunset
Gentle fading colors
Reaching towards land's horizon
Searching for a new palate
To wash its brush upon.

Fences

Fences

Shrouded fences, morning fog
Amid dry cornstalks silent, still
Claim their gnarled, aged right
Stand by sheer determined will.

Sunshine struggles through the mist
Moonsets in dark western skies
Fences, barrier's vigil keep
Birds awake, but do not fly.

Noon comes with autumnal blaze
Ancient beam-posts fields still part
Heavy briars of former days
Burden fences and weathered hearts.

Life will blow its breath across
Prairie's edge in shining sun
Soften visions of things once lost
God tears down fences
One
By
One.

Be Careful What You Pray For

My mother told me to be careful what you pray for, and as usual, she was right.

On a recent day, I was working outside and feeling rather pensive, thinking about my answered prayer, as pile of wood burned brightly near the field, and the sun shone upon the early spring grass.

Springtime in the Midwest can be eventful, and eleven months ago, during the prior spring, our family huddled together, terrified, on the basement floor. I prayed. The sound of a freight train rumbled all around us, the house shuddered as the sucking blackness of a storm enveloped the house. I felt the ground shaking beneath us, and the ferocious wind roared, as I have never heard before. I recited The Lord's Prayer as I held my child, and then asked Him to please spare our lives from this tornado, and if He had to take anything, please let it be the old barn, not our 120 year-old farm-home. For a moment the rumbling ceased, but then started again, on the other side of our house.

He gave me what I asked for.

After the storm, we emerged from the cellar, and witnessed the biggest mess I have ever seen. It was not a huge tornado, nor a completely destructive one, yet cornstalks were strewn like a carpet over the yard, many baby birds and their parents dismembered and scattered about, trees torn and uprooted, with a path carved in the woods behind our property. A 90 year-old fir tree was ripped out of the ground, and thrown on our roof, grazing the side of the house. But the barn was still standing, at first glance. The old hayloft door was blown open, and the entry doors were blown off. Well, maybe that can be fixed, we thought. Upon further examination, however, my husband and I saw the old barn had been lifted and shifted off its foundation, which had crumbled underneath the weight. Now, the barn must be torn down, it was dangerously leaning over and beyond repair.

I don't know when it was built, but I would guess around WWII, when farm life had not completely faded from the American lifestyle. I often imagined what it might have been like within the interior; chestnut colored horses and painted green hayracks of yesteryear waiting a day's work, the smell of sweet alfalfa, shelled corn, and the crow of a rooster greeting the dawn. When we bought this property, we painted the barn bright red, so bright that you could see it for miles. We were remodeling our house also, and removed the old steep stairway, installing it within the barn to reach the loft. Concrete poured for the foundation was riddled with stones, and the beams were scant 2 x 4's nailed together. There was a pulley and rail at the peak of the barn for moving hay bales up and into the storage loft, for cattle that used to live in the stalls below. The upper rail was put on the top beam with square nails, and there were a few older pieces of lumber full cut and rough-hewn. Perhaps, it was recycled from another, older building on the property. There have been many buildings upon this land, come and gone. We used the barn for storage, a place to park the tractor, and a general parts supply shop. It was a useful barn in its time, and now, that time was over.

So the other day, as I was helping to finally clean it up, I discovered treasures in the rubble: iron shoes from draft horses, an old medicine bottle, electric insulators, and choice pieces of barn siding I would save for other projects, someday. As my husband used the tractor to it all haul away, the area still carried aromas of cats and mice, old dust, dirt and oil, and soft clumps of moss, which grew on the north side in the ever constant, wet shade. The sky would never again reflect on the foursquare windowpanes its dazzling white clouds set amid an expanse of turquoise blue. My husband pulled our old stairway to the burn pile when I was not watching. Somehow I had dreamed it might be used again someday, somewhere. Along with the history, it was gone in five minutes amid the dancing orange flames.

I feel the loss of an old relationship, and something is now missing from my life. The old barn would greet me in the early morning, the sun shining through her windowpanes from east to west, her siding glowing red and vibrant. Like an aged wrinkled lady, she still smiled everyday. The cats would dart in and out of her warped siding as if it was an old skirt, chase the mice, and play games before stopping to nap in a sunny spot on the wind protected south side. I come home in the evening and still see her shadow in the black of night, the peak of the loft rising towards the stars, the moonlight shining from her tin roof, and owls harboring within the safety of her trusses. The image is burnt in my memory, branded upon my mind in colors of dark crimson and shining silver, with the sound of her frame creaking slowly in the wind. Now, what is left of her will become paneling for a family room, or picture frames, or maybe just a remembrance within this book.

A hundred years from now, no one will know what was missed by not seeing the barn. Someday, even the memory will fade, and this book will become dust. Just as I look out on the fields and sometimes wonder what the Potawatomies thought when we plowed the tall grass prairies under, the buffalo left, and the songbird flew away. I will never experience a beautiful sea of gold flecked with wildflowers red and blue, stretching out for hundreds of miles, moving in perfect unison with the wind. And a hundred years from now, someone else will have to imagine my red barn of yesteryear, the fresh smell of hay, moonlight reflecting off the roof, and the crow of a rooster at dawn. It has all gone to the wind.

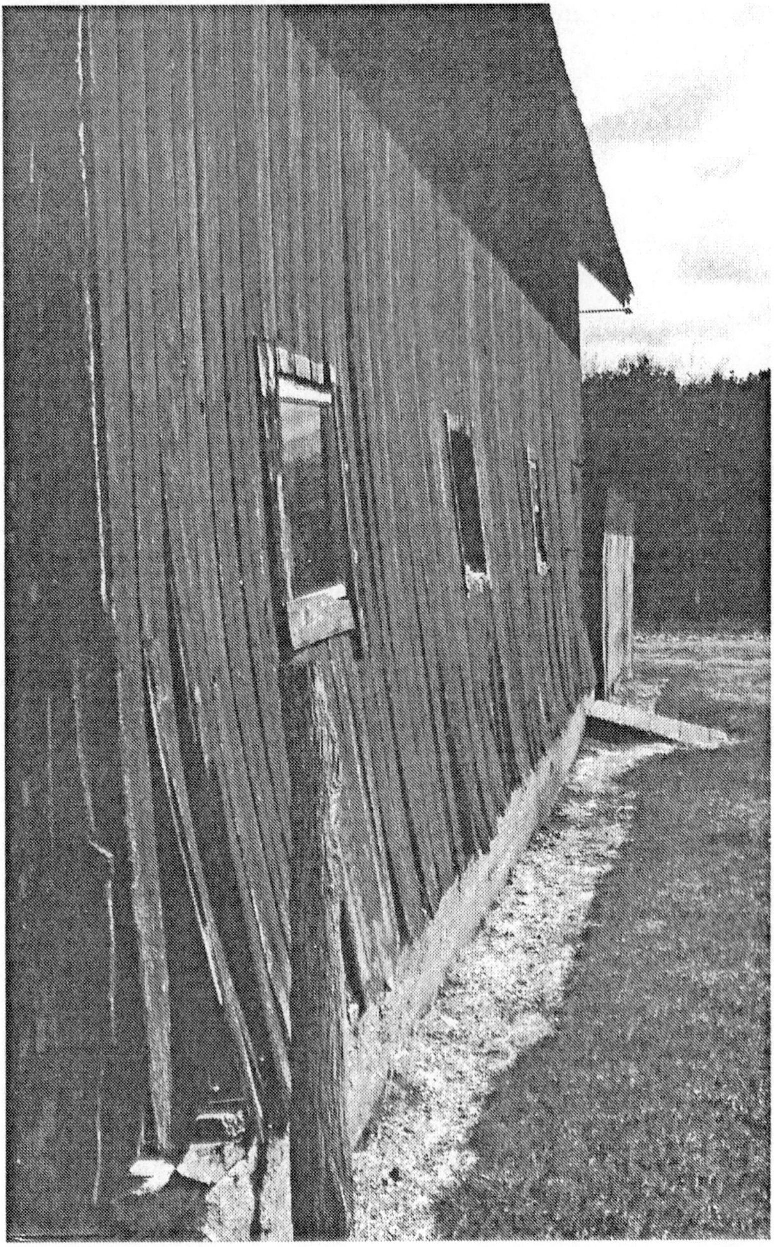

Barn

Proud
And still
Standing tall
A survivor upon a landscape
Where winter winds ravage
Boards warped
And summer sun bakes
Curling paint peeled
And birds build
Rafter nests in the eaves.
Alone
As a reminder
Of realities gone by
And sweet green fragrance mowed in spring.
A memory of what was
And a promise
Of what is to be.
It stands
Waiting
For the turn of the times.

The Gift

You gave me
Dappled painted sunsets
Wind whispers
Green through trembling trees
I see You
In every blazon
Autumn gold
Hear You
In every birdsong
Morning in spring
Feel Your touch
In drifting winds
And sunshine warm
Upon my smile.

The Compass

Partial
Full moon
Evening sky
Gaze upward
If you try
You can see
Our stars

Sharp

Life
Has chiseled me
Sharp around the edges
With slices of insight
Drilled down to the truth.
But
My dear friend
I will let you hold my soul
Like a shimmering sky diamond
Covered with night's black velvet
Unwrap me like a package
And see
Who I truly am
Behind my veil of uncertainty
And distrust
And self-preservation.
Underneath
I am really just plain carbon
Protected by sharp edges
Created over time.
Call my bluff.
Please.

Lost in the Desert

Broken branches
Stretch dying
To crackled skies
Blazon orange
Dust blowing
To another time.
Oasis search
Only a mirage
In the distance.
Vultures soar
Waiting…
As a hawk perches
In the tree.

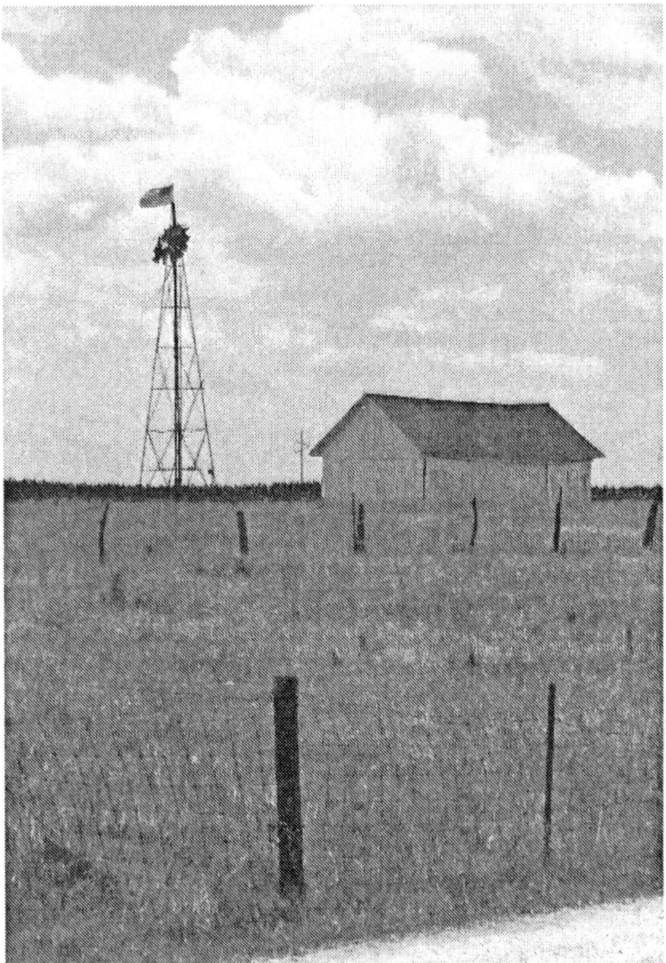

Things Left Behind

It was foggy this morning. The mist hung damp and still, making wet everything it touched, blurring images of homes, barns, and trees from reality, as a blue-gray veil hung over the morning horizon, creating a surrealistic view of the landscape. The encroaching subdivisions in the distance almost disappeared from view-almost.

There are places I miss, and I haven't even moved anywhere. I thought that living in the same place for so long, would assure me my surroundings would remain unchanged. Not so. I have lived in this county for 20 years, and I drive to work 12 miles every day across the countryside. I love the rolling land, the various multi-color morning sunrises, and the rural atmosphere. But I look at the empty spaces where a favorite barn or homestead used to stand, and feel a void inside of me where joy used to linger as I passed those old places. Sometimes just the trees remain, or sometimes, nothing. Or worse, it is completely gone and cookie cutter houses have taken over.

You see no one cares anymore. Not really. The old homesteads and barns are rapidly disappearing from our area. The reasons vary; they are stolen from the land by age and neglect, or because no one wants the responsibility of their care anymore. Or, they succumb to Midwest storms, which can be unforgiving. Or, they are taken by greed for money, masked in the light of progress. I think mostly it is the latter. But no one cares enough to stop it, nor do they have the energy to fight greed.

What used to be family farms are almost extinct. Any place near the edge of the city is annexed involuntarily into it, swallowed up by the plague of progress, or taxed so high that a person cannot afford to stay. Selling it and giving in is easier and cheaper, and those who leave it are either dead, or making way to less crowded pastures. The lure of the almighty dollar is stronger than any sentiment, or historical appeal, or lifestyle.

So I drive through the country, feeling old. Just like a grandmother who talks about a farm that used to exist on a particular section of land, only I can see what used to be. My child will never see it. And I will bore him with my conversation as older people can do to young ones. Time will blur my memories, like the fog does the landscape. And maybe, over time, I will forget some things. But, when I drive by a place, or have a moment that reminds me of somewhere long gone, that empty feeling remains. I don't think any amount of time, or fog, will take that reality from me. It does make me wonder where our values lie as a people. Perhaps those too, have become foggy, shrouded in veils of progress. Or maybe, no one cares beyond the personal political agendas, for the common good and spirit of what we used to be.

How to Dress for Snow Play

In Colorado:

Get up late morning, have cappuccino while enjoying the mountain view, shower with designer bath gel, use matching perfume, put on make-up, and fix hair nicely

Put on long silk underwear, leggings, and socks from upscale mail-order catalog

Clothe in a one-piece designer ski outfit purchased in Aspen

Finish with genuine antelope boots trimmed with Navajo beads

Don't forget lightweight cashmere lined gloves, which match the clothes, and sunglasses

Gracefully waltz outside

In the Midwest:

Get up early before the snowplows make a mess of things

Forget the shower, just brush the hair, skip the deodorant, no make-up, no perfume

Dress in dime store variety cotton underwear

Put on farm store long johns—top and bottom

Start on first layer of socks

Follow with second layer of socks

Cover in large blue jeans—an old pair to fit over bottom long johns

Pull turtleneck over top half of long johns—okay to get from dirty laundry
Peel on wool sweater
Top with down jacket—old one
Pull over all, ski type bib overalls—farm store brand
Step into snow jogger boots, plastic kind with foam liners
Finish this with heavy duty wind breaker that has a hood
Wrap scarf around neck, to hide lower part of face
Place stocking cap on head
Tie hood tightly over hair and stocking cap
Put on glove liners
Cover them with farm chore gloves
Waddle outside
As the cold air hits you, remember you forgot to go to the bathroom
Reverse, give up, and go take a shower

Keeping Up

Stuck in the shallows
Stubbornness of spirit
Denies depth
Self-righteousness rules
Ailing actions
As you struggle for surface
To make it all look right.
Hardness of heart
Will only drown you in the end.
Perhaps
It is time
For a change.

Working

I hated it for years. Getting up early, for any reason, and especially driving to work. The drudgery, the bleary eyed feeling. And then, today, something dawned on me. This too, is a gift. Wow. I am serious. A gift. There are gifts hidden in everything, even that which seems unacceptable or a burden.

You see, the mornings are beautiful in the country. Today the rising sun was shining through a misty haze, across fields glowing green in the light. The trees dotting the countryside were deep emerald, refreshed after a night's rest. Birds were singing everywhere, flitting in and out of the tall fescue grass growing in the ditches, and streams trickled along the sides of the fields. Tall yellow daisies nodded their heads towards the sun, growing among the spiky cattails anchored in the mud. Purple wildflowers thick along the back edge of the ditch, gave a perfectly contrasting backdrop for the other foliage. The birds were celebrating in unison; flowers danced in the breeze, as the sun was rising through the mist. It was a new day, and a new beginning.

The morning is also when I do most of my writing. Driving in the car by myself, out in the country, my spirit opens up and reaches from horizon to horizon, and words seem to create themselves. So I suppose I cannot take much credit for my writing. It is a gift of the morning, a gift from the Creator. It is something for me to share with you for His glory, and purpose, and the dawn of a new day.

Canvas

I no longer recognize
Hellos
Or Goodbyes
Hellos hold too many promises
Goodbyes too final
For my fragile heart.
So my life
Has become
Like a canvas
Painted upon from one edge to another
Held by the shoulders of God.
Each encounter and experience
Melting into another
As if one continuous
Comet tail
Streaking across the sky.

Cosmetic Surgery

I loved everything about the old house, even though others didn't. It possessed a character that can only be achieved over years, a feeling that instantly surrounded you in history from another era. We lived there for 15 years, with some improvements along the way, but never to the degree that it interfered with the dignity of the simple, old lady.

Cracked horsehair lathe-n-plaster walls were etched with traces of an artist's trowel work from another time, and I had memorized every crack, every stroke of the metal trowel as it had attempted to make things smooth. Trim around the doors and windows were chipped and timeworn, painted with layers of different colors; leaving evidence everywhere of other lives that passed through the hall-less home. The doors squeaked as they hung on their flowered, cast iron hinges, white porcelain knobs were mounted halfway down the side, and I managed to lock myself out of a room or two, due to the box locks located on only one side of the doors. The wide plank wooden floors would creak only in certain places, so you could tell exactly where someone was within the house, like an audio map in your mind. Windows rattled in the wind as a weather indicator, and feathered frost graced the panes during winter. Wainscoting was present in the dining room and kitchen, and the kitchen floorboards boasted wear and tear around the chimney, evidence of a woodstove and a heavily used area. You could almost smell the fried chicken, homemade pickles, and baked pies.

It wasn't perfect, but really nothing ever is. The house still stood straight and tall, even after 120 years. A man named Edgar built it. He was a farmer, a schoolteacher, and a husband to an Italian wife. They had four children, and many grandchildren. One grandchild made a visit to me one day when she was 89. I learned about her family, and history of the home that only she would know. She lived there one year and told me of family picnics and events held at the farm; her brother's wedding, Indian arrowheads found near the creek, and how the house fell out of the family's ownership.

The house had a voice all its own, a character like wrinkled faces and old eyes, reflecting a history of its journey through time. A history, which was stripped out of it, piece-by-piece, board-by-board, one square nail at a time. I loved that house, and now, it is like a death of an old friend. The character has changed. The structure, and some original lathe and plaster are hidden behind the new walls, with smells of paint and varnish permeating the house. Yes, it looks very nice, but I don't feel at home anymore. This doesn't feel right at all. I suppose I will get used to it.

But yesterday, I noticed a crack in the new drywall, located where an old one used to be. Perhaps the house is still speaking after all. Even through her face has changed you cannot silence her soul. Underneath all the cosmetic surgery she is still there, telling stories of the past, her beams standing tall in the Illinois wind, and her voice, whispering in my ear.

Sea

Sea
She trembles from afar
A whispered voice beckons
To come and touch her shore
Where rock and sand
Meet and tumble
Together
And a traveler can rest
From weariness
In the cradle
Of her longing arms.

Sea
She dances waiting
Singing to the sun
Drifting up and down
To the horizon
And back
Moving in and out
Over the sand
Searching for her lost one.

Sea
She rejoices laughing
In glistened sparkled foam
And froth
And hushing
Of her breaking waves
Meeting once again
The endless yearning
Of her calling heart
Where dreams balance
On the edge
Of infinity.

Prisoner by Design

You are a prisoner
Here
Truth was not your rudder
And your dreams
Like winds full of promise
Have blown you
To a far away shore
An unexpected place
Of confusion
And regret
And longing
An island of no return
A place from where you gaze
On distant horizons.
You are a prisoner here
By your own design.

Lost and Found

Lonely moon
Shine bright
In darkened skies
Slowly rise
Secrets reflecting
In your pale golden face.
Woo me
Coo me melodies
To sooth my heart
Sparking new dreams
With dancing stars
Trailing silvery tails
And wishes
Across the evening sky.

I know you
As I should
But now how I want
Maybe that means
Your reality is
Not to my best interest
When slowly I feel myself
Knowing you more
And me less.

Like others
You will take her home
Culture her style
With cabernets
And music.
I am just another number
In your book
To call in moments of loneliness
And the need of understanding.
Still,
I feel like a cup of cold coffee
Discarded and grumbled at
By a man
Who refuses to understand the temperature.
I wonder if
You will ever rise
Above
Your own insecurities
And reach beyond
What a bedroom brings you.

Images

Seals
Silky brown
Harping
Bounding down
Towards a chilly blue sea
Aleutians
I'm dreaming
Magical pictures painting
A bridge
From imaginary colors
Wandering
Towards distant islands.
Sometimes
You are so far away
It seems
All that's left of you
Are dreams.

Hood

Majestic
Snow white
Cragged peaks
Sticking skyward
My God
Made this mountain
Upon where
Beauty shines back
In the face of the sun.

Prophecy

Faded dreams preserved within
Thoughts mirrored with my sighs
Saving them for shining stars
Reminiscent of your eyes
All for another time.

A Long Way from Palos Verdes

I was a long way from the place of my dreams as I sat on my camp chair in the blazing 102-degree sun, trying to imagine anywhere but where I was. I was hot, sweaty, and miserable. We were camping and I was trying to be a good sport, but camping was never my first choice of a "vacation." My camping experience had been limited to being in the California redwoods which carry the fragrance of pine and moss, as stillness hangs amid the rays of filtered light through 2000 year old trees, or along the coast of Half Moon Bay, the ocean lulling me to sleep at night, the salty air fresh and crisp, and the cry of seagulls gracing the morning sunrise.

But this was different. So, to distract my mind I thought of my former camping experiences, and Palos Verdes, where I used to live. Its lush green hills roll to cliffs that jut above the whispering sea, and Santa Catalina Island shimmers in the distance. It is cool there most of the year, and right now, a world away. There are moments in your life you question the sanity of your decisions, and this was one of them.

I was not a kidnap victim, but a reluctant participant in this Midwest camping adventure. Everyone wanted to go, except me. But, I decided to be a good sport and try it. I was told they had a pool there, others volunteered to do all the cooking, and this camping trip would be a lot of FUN.

We traveled six hours by car, and arrived at a theme-oriented campground late at night, shortly after a "cooling rainfall," but the air still hung thick and sticky. Driving over some railroad tracks just off the main highway, all of us were greeted by a fiberglass statue of Mr. Bear waving 'hello'. Colorful theme oriented decorations abounded all over the campground, like plastic lawn ornaments. We were told there was a pool for swimming, a general store, and "modern" showers. We set up camp in the dark, and after what seemed like hours of exact engineering and research on the proper place to drive the stakes, pitched the tent. However, the dew point that evening was 75 degrees, and the humidity permeated everything, the air, the tent, me. My son asked me "Mommy, why are the pillows wet?" as he lay down to sleep. "Never mind" I answered, "Just go to sleep." I listened to the hum of our electric fan and closed my eyes. The tent felt like a Slow Cooker getting ready for an overnight bake. I was tired and figured that in spite of the dampness and sticky warmth of the night, I could fall asleep. Still, I wanted an air conditioner and dry sheets. Mr. Bear did not provide those. Little did I know that my adventure was just beginning.

I was barely dozing off, and heard what sounded like thunderstorm coming. Oh joy, to add to my hot and sticky camping experience, a drenching rainstorm. But I was wrong. It was our new friend, Mr. Freight Train. Funny, how the campground did not advertise Mr. Freight Train, or paint little smiling faces of him anywhere at the site. We were camped under some trees, near the tracks, so we got to experience the excitement and train noise barreling in from the distance, shaking the tent. To add more joy, it is required of course to blast that darn whistle at the entrance to the park. And to make sure we did not forget how much fun it could be, the train visited us four times that night, every two hours. In between his visits, Mr. Semi Truck and his companions passed on the main highway, which we were also in close proximity to, every five minutes. However, I still held hope in my heart that we were going to have FUN.

The campground managers told us after two nights we would have to move from our campsite to another one. What was so special about this spot, that someone reserved it long ago? Upon waking at sunrise, I realized why. We were under one of the few trees in the campground—and the other sites were in the full blazing sunlight. Enter Mr. & Mrs. Pseudo Canine and their pup family. The squatters jealously guarded all shady spots. Evil eye looks were given to you if you stared longingly at their tree. The campground was crowded like a can of sardines, each camper neatly tucked into their 10 x 20 foot allotted space, which were marked with site numbers on top of colorfully painted smiling bear poles, and electrical outlets perched on top of a metal stick. Many campsites were decorated with multi-colored fish and flower lights strung across imaginary barriers in between their precious trees. I had never seen so many people crowded into such a small area.

I checked out the "modern" restrooms. My Junior High school locker room was cleaner. The newest decorating trend was Toilet Paper Streamers, conveniently held to the floor by old soap and shampoo. Of course, the campground managers wanted to let everyone know how stylish their customers were, so in order to pull that one off, the Toilet Paper Streamers also stuck to the bottom of your shower shoes (you don't DARE go in without them). Many a camper was seen exiting the bathroom and shower area with streamers of the latest fashionable item trailing behind them. I decided then and there that it was no place for a shower, and I would avoid one as long as I could. Being smelly was no worse than being a fashion statement for Mr. Bear's campground.

Well since we were there, this also meant a trip to the gift shop. Not too bad of a place, if you wanted an expensive little reminder of a "vacation," which consisted of a smiling plastic Mr. Bear key ring at $19.95 plus tax. I looked for Mr. Freight Train accessories, but alas, there were none. There were however, rolls of toilet paper for sale, why I do not know. There seemed to be more than plenty to go around.

Being rather disappointed in the gift shop, we decided a dip in the pool would be nice. During the summer of 1999, the Midwest was breaking all heat records in history. A cool dip in a clear blue pool sounded nice, and besides, I could hear the happy yelps from the Pseudo Canine Family on the other side of the fence, and the kids were anxious to go. So…we did.

Welcome to The Hog Wallow. The water was pea-green and not at all clear. The pool was crowded beyond capacity—the campers were all grunting and squealing happily, soggy diapered bottoms and baby oil floating on top of the water in between the beach balls and various other floating toys. Oh joy, just what I wanted. Where was that clear blue pool I was promised? I opted for a suntan and ice tea instead.

That night our Slow Cooker was again hot and muggy, with a high dew point in the air. I don't even remember what we had for dinner. A costumed Mr. Bear waved, and held a parade down the middle of the camp road, complete with Mr. Cat, Baby Bear, Doggie and his Daddy, and the camping families happily riding on top of a hay wagon being pulled by an old swayback Nellie of a horse. Well at least we would go to another campsite tomorrow, maybe further away from the tracks. Mr. Freight Train came twice that night, and Mr. Semi all night long. I was still hot. I still wanted an air conditioner. I still hadn't taken a shower.

We broke camp (see I am getting the lingo here) in the morning, and proceeded to transfer our tent, chairs, tables, sleeping bags, blankets, sheets, coolers, camp table, rugs, camp mattresses, pillows, food, toys, electric fans, clothes, clothesline, and bodies over to the new site. Oh joy, it was in the blazing sun, not a teeny tiny tree in site, and it was 90 degrees at 10 a.m. But to look on the brighter side, it was not next to Mr. Freight Train and his tracks, or the main highway with its parade of trucks.

The kids were begging to go swimming in the pool. They didn't care if it was pea green. But I could not get myself to get in it. Between the Toilet Paper Streamers stuck to shower shoes, and the floating pool toys, it was all I could do to drink my tea. TEA?! "What am I thinking?" I asked myself as I watched the kids play. I needed something stronger, colder, and within air conditioning! We went back to the campground to relax and eat lunch. The heat was getting to me. I was sitting in the blazing sun, and the heat index was 115. My sun hat helped some, but mainly was used to hide my unkempt hair. I was melting and having delusional daydreams of Palos Verdes, the Sierras, and the ocean, ANYWHERE BUT THE CAMPGROUND. It then dawned on me. I need to get in where it was cool. I actually felt ill. So I stated simply "I am feeling sick from this heat, I need air conditioning, ANYWHERE, and I don't care where." They knew I was serious.

We walked through the nearby woods, and found a quiet little restaurant/bar complete with 1955 metal tables and peeling, cigarette burnt linoleum flooring of the same vintage. Inside the air was cool. AHHHH. The establishment served cheeseburgers that were fried in a kitchen, not in the sun, video games for the kids stood against the walls, and they served cold beer. I didn't care how many quarters the kids invested into the video games. So what if it cost 100 dollars an hour to finance their fun? We stayed there until 5pm, when the evening crowd came in and we deemed it too wild for the kids to be around. I was sad to leave the air conditioning. Gazing at the little mom-n-pop motel across road, it looked good; air conditioners stuck out of the windows, rusty cars were parked in front, and crooked wooden stairs led to each cubicle of a room. I am sure they also had vintage linoleum floors, grandma's chenille spreads, and an ashtray in every corner. I suppose I could survive for one more night. I was dirty and tired but tomorrow we were going to a hotel. That was my only hope.

Back at the campsite, we decided to make S'mores. You know, that concoction of toasted marshmallows, graham crackers, and chocolate bars that everyone else raves about. I was in charge of 'cooking' them. Oh joy, as I opened the chocolate bars, all I found was a gooey, sticky, pile of brown that was permanently stuck to the paper. Perfect for fondue, if you happened to have a fondue pot. Our friends went to the general store and bought fresh chocolate bars. I helped make the S'mores, and graciously gave one to my son, telling him it was a real camping treat, trying to be positive. My son took one bite and said, "I don't like it. It tastes yucky." and then "Mommy I am HOT." It was 7pm and still 90 degrees. I got my shower shoes, and rinsed off in the Toilet Paper Streamer Gallery, trying to make my hair look civilized. I had a cold beer. Okay, more than one.

That evening Mr. Freight Train and Mr. Semi roared in the distance. Mr. Bear held a parade, his friends and companions followed him around. He had new riders for his hayrack, and Old Nel' led the way. Our tent was a Slow Cooker on the 'high' setting, in spite of our fan blowing hot air on us. Happy squeals and yelps could be heard from The Hog Wallow. The Toilet Paper Streamer Gallery was giving tours. I was ready to go to a hotel.

The next night we checked into a hotel that sat on a harbor overlooking an inlet to Lake Michigan. If it had cost $2000 a night, I wouldn't have cared. Beautiful sailboats and yachts of every size filled its pristine clean docks. On the boardwalk sat round tables shaded by umbrellas and flanked by upholstered chairs. Each table was complete with fresh flowers in a vase, and two families were having afternoon strawberries, and champagne chilled in a sterling silver bucket. Hotel linens were crisp, the room was cool, and I had fluffy pillows to sleep on. The pool was a perfect temperature, the hot tub bubbling, and a restaurant was on-site. No trains, no trucks, no Mr. Bear and his companions, no Hog Wallow, no Slow Cooker, no multi-colored lawn decorations, and no Toilet Paper Streamer Gallery. I told my husband I am never camping again.

The next day, we arrived back at our house, and discovered the solar cover on our pool had melted due to the hot sun and heat. I guess I should have stayed home.

Undoing

It is
The doings
And un-doings
Of everyday
Opening and closing
Sunset and moonrise
Playing in puddles muddy
Then laundry on the floor
Anymore
Life is messy.

Doings and un-doings
Of us
Moments of delight
And remorse
And puzzlement
Discoveries
Of our own doings and un-doings
Each day muddled from a past
And a future moving
In perpetual motion.
Relationships are messy.

Doings and un-doings
Of my heart
Once held in your hand
Trusting and hopeful now gone
With the moonsets and dirty laundry
Broken beliefs
And dreams upon the floor

Anymore
They're just empty words
Promises broken and excuses delivered
You see
What's left of me
You can't reach.
That was your un-doing.

Connie

Strange, how aromas can bring back vivid memories of your past. It could be the fragrance of someone's perfume, a flower, a fresh mown lawn or hayfield, or the sticky wet tar-like smell of pavement after a good summer rain in the city. They all seem to evoke our memories, and take us back to a different place and time, even if for only a moment.

And so it is for me when I smell uncooked rice. Every time I smell rice, it reminds me of Connie. When she was married, the ushers gave out little packets of rice wrapped in bridal tulle and tied with pretty satin ribbons. Back in the 1960's it was a long standing tradition and considered good luck for rice to be thrown at the bride and groom after the ceremony.

I must have been four years old, or five at the most when Connie was our babysitter. I had two sisters, one older, one younger and still an infant. Not really aware of my parent's work schedule, all I knew was if Mom or Dad were not going to be home, or if they were going out for dinner without us (to a someplace very BORING), Connie would come and stay with us.

It was 1962, I think, or maybe '63. She was young, probably 19 or 20 years of age, and had dark, dark hair. I always thought she was so pretty, wanted to be like her, and she reminded me of the ever so popular TV star of the time, Annette Funicello from the Mickey Mouse Club.

Connie was gentle and kind. She would read us stories and play games with us, hug us when we needed it, and break up the sister fights while toting baby sister on her hip. She would cook something good to eat when we were hungry, and when naughty she had a way of corralling us kids into some alternative activity. But she never reported our behavior if we were bad or misbehaving. She would just state we were "wound up" or something else that sounded politically politely correct. Connie was fun, pretty, loving, and we trusted her.

One day, Mom announced that Connie was getting married. "Cool," I thought, imagining her in a big white dress looking like a princess wearing a crown. MY Connie, getting to be a star for a day! My mother told me this meant she would not baby-sit us any more. That dampened my spirit for the whole event, and I became very sad. We were all so comfortable with her, and did not understand how she would LEAVE us. After all, she was a part of our family, or so I felt at such a young age. I guess my mother could see the distress on my face, and she tried to explain to me that Connie was going to get married, and have her own babies to take care of. "Why can't she bring them to our house?" I asked. It seemed the perfect solution to me. Mom tried to explain the cooking, cleaning, diapering, household management and general responsibilities of being a wife and mother to me. It was just too hard for a young child to comprehend. I simply just had to accept it that was all.

Bless Connie that she invited the whole family to her wedding. Fidgety kids and weddings don't mix too well, but she loved us and so we went. It was a full Catholic mass, I think, and I remember getting particularly wiggly and my mother getting tired of me acting so. Connie looked absolutely beautiful, walking down the aisle in a full white dress, flowers being carried in her hand as a traditional rendition of "Here Comes The Bride" was played on the organ. I held the little rice packet tightly in my hand, trying to entertain myself in an endless delivery of sermons and vows. I kept sniffing the rice packet, thought how good it smelled, played with the ribbon, and picked on the tulle. Afterwards, Connie introduced us to her family and husband. She was so proud and looked bigger than life in her wedding gown, and I felt so small and insignificant standing next to her. It was like a page being turned in a storybook right before my eyes, and I had no control over anything, anymore. I just wanted her to hold me one more time, eat the hot dogs she cooked for dinner, and tell me she would come for a visit, sometime. She never did. She had a new life.

I am sure that she was a wonderful mother. I hope she had many happy years with a family, because she gave me so much in the little time spent with us. Someone like that deserves happiness. I suppose she would be about 62 or so now. Hard to imagine, because I still see her dark hair and fair face as being 20 years old, fresh and untouched by life. If I had a chance, I would like to thank her for being there when my parents could not; being kind, loving, gentle, cooking me meals and snacks, and giving me wonderful memories of someone I could trust with my feelings and fears.

But since I can't, I think I will cook rice for dinner tonight. I wonder if she remembers me.

The Wedding

Winter arrived late last night
In a wedding gown
Of softly falling fluffy white
Nestled on the ground.

She awoke crimson, blushing
Color rising in the west
Her dazzling sequins pink and gold
Sewn upon her vest.

Midnight blue fading thin
She left it in the east
A breezy skirt brushed up the snow
An airborne crystal feast.

A blushing veil, a wafting hem,
In early morning's light,
Then in a fairy instant- Poof!
It changed to brilliant white.

Old Windows

I can sleep through the ceaseless Midwest wind, now. But it wasn't always that way. The 100 year-old windows that graced our simple farmhouse made sure of that, and I loved them in spite of their inefficiency. Like shining eyes of an old lady, shown to me through the glass was life, full of wisdom and wonder, changing with the seasons.

The old wooden windows rattled in the wind and I could tell just how bad an incoming storm was by the frequency of shaking frames. If the sound pitch reached a rapid beat, I knew it was time to open the basement door for a quick descent to escape a potentially deadly storm, or if in winter, put on the goose down comforter, and not worry about the haunting howl of wind whipping its way across the plains.

Wintertime created beautiful works of art on the 2 over 2 windowpanes. Frost always made a new pattern, never the same. Sometimes it looked like veined leaves of summer trees, or geometric patterns similar to art by Salvador Dali, and sometimes petals of flower patterns clung to the glass. It was always a fascination to see what teasing gift Jack Frost would leave overnight, and how the circling sun would glow through the glass during the day, and melt it all away into drips and puddles that settled on the ancient sills.

In spring and summer, I would gaze out of the hand blown glass, and the world outside would give a rippled reflection back to me. Outside details were not visible, only a wiggly-watery image of moving colors and shapes viewed through bubbles blown with breath long since gone. Only seven panes of original glass remained from years of tenant occupation, but I often imagined what the original builders saw when the house was new. The sashes left plenty of room for spider nests and drafts, frost and ice, and ever-cracking caulk, but it certainly was a vast improvement for the 1870's and still, I loved them anyway.

But they were inefficient. Sash weights were cut in some, and you had to prop them open with a short metal bolt, or a tall wooden stick, depending on the amount of air movement desired within the room. The winter wind was unstoppable, filtering in with a sharp frigid bite through every single crack, capable of bringing down the temperature rapidly all over the house, and keeping the 40-year old oil furnace constantly humming. Trim around the windows was wide and plain, and had been painted many, many times over the years, probably with lead paint under the innermost layers. They were drafty, noisy, and imperfect.

Yet, I could hear the birds sing in the morning, hear the wind, smell the fresh mown hay as it was cut from the horse pasture next door. However, the heating bills were too high, and the cost of replacing the windows would outshine the heating bills in five years, so we installed new ones. We gained a lower heat bill, a much, *much* warmer house, and a quiet stillness that was almost a noise in itself, setting me apart from my world, not being part of it anymore. I lost the storm gauge, Jack Frost's indoor art, melodic morning birdsong, and the fragrance of sweet cut alfalfa. The price to pay for progress, I suppose. Something lost, something gained. But it will never be the same.

The windows went on the community sale and brought $5.00, all 22 of them.

Most people don't like old things.

The Search

Beauty exists
Far away from your cities
On mountain snow
Moonlit glow
In blue
Silence
Your soul
Great Creator speaks
In stillness
Listen
And quiet the noise
Of your mind.

Firebird

Awaken Phoenix
Arise from ashes
To glimpse a new day
Flames have died
You paid the price
With your heart
And soul now standing
As silver refined
In fire
Dawn has come
You have just begun
To love
Rejoice
You have been given life
Again.

Sunrise

Like a misty opal jewel
The morning comes
So with the sun
The stillness hangs
Amidst dew-gemmed fields
And silent trees
Awakened
By a chorus of wings
And song
And life's sweet breath
Of a new day.

Wondering

And we wonder why the children are afraid.

I had the good and unusual fortune of being raised by conservative Midwest parents on the California coast. We had picnics among redwoods near craggy cliffs, and tide pool outings at Half Moon Bay. Our entertainment was restricted to the parks, the attic filled with toys, our own backyard, and imaginations. Television viewing was minimal, and when we did watch it, it was limited to music shows, Disney, or situation comedies of the era. Westerns, spooky subjects, and detective shows were off limits to us.

We were not allowed to watch "monster movies." They gave us nightmares. Never mind that the primitive Japanese animation looked silly compared to now, or we were told it wasn't real. It was simply the terror of other people acting scared that raised alarm within us. Just the thought of something trying to eat you alive was evil, let alone any spilled blood or hysterical women screaming for a hero to save them. My parents thought we should not be conditioned into enjoying the adrenaline rush of panic, terror, or mayhem.

As years went by, the cinema's movie animation progressed to gory saliva slime drenched creatures straight from Hell. The producers gave them ratings, PG or PG 13. Well-meaning parents let their children see them, under the guise of "its just science fiction" or "its not real," or "my child is mature enough to know the difference." It was advanced monster movies set for teens.

Eventually however, the thrill of the sci-fi movies wears off as being stupid or babyish, even to teenagers. Enter the terror of ghoulish human fiends, slasher movies, twisted demented people who stalk and hack some innocent person to death. Again, we tell people "its not real, its entertainment." It is entertainment on a level of horror.

We as people, and a society have become numb. After all, it's only pretend, right? Or is it?

I have learned that what we occupy our thoughts with is what we eventually become. Our environment, however trivial or imaginary we may think it to be, influences us all. We are only human beings, with feelings and thoughts, and, sensitivities to be reckoned with. I turned on the TV news the other night. The top stories were of; an at-large serial killer who travels the rails, a mother who tried to discreetly poison her child's bottle, and a politician caught in lewd and despicable acts.

The monsters have evolved. Evolved from thoughts, to words, to numbness, to actions that we do not take responsibility for. After all, it's not our fault. It is the environment. But, it is one we have created. We tell ourselves it is upbringing, lack of morals, guidance, but do nothing to improve the environment, except to legislate people's actions, without cleaning up the filth around them. It is filth, which cannot be avoided, even if we tell our kids "don't touch." They will follow our example, no matter what we say otherwise.

So we wonder why the children are afraid. It is because now, the monsters are real. And they know it.

Just in Passing

I guess I must be slow on some things. As you now realize, I contemplate life and all of its intricate dynamics, trying to figure them out in my own mind, and letting God show me realizations, within His own time, when He feels I can handle it.

Wow, tonight it hit me like a ton of bricks.

I was thoroughly enjoying my son's choral concert at school, reminiscing about my own childhood choral concerts, how I thought we sounded professional, and how my parents were so proud of me. The music teacher is wonderful, and she has worked hard with the kids to teach them about music, that it is a living, breathing art form expressed in sounds, which fall upon our ears and hearts. I was thinking how fleeting childhood is, and seeing those children up on stage, you almost see their future faces, vocations, and dreams as they danced and swayed with the music. I was simply full of smiles.

After the concert we went home, to our old farmhouse, its antiquities strewn about in a mish-mash of mess due to constant remodeling. I love old things; the artistry that went into them is not present in anything you can buy now from a run-of-the-mill department store. Everything now seems to be mass-produced, all looking like rubber stamps of each other. I even like the chipped paint, dented cupboard doors, and rusty spots on my antiques, strange as it may seem. It is testimony of other people and places that came before me, people who lived, struggled, laughed and loved, are now long gone.

There is an expression of speech that nothing lasts forever, that all *things* are temporary. But I look at these antique things; some having been around for over 200 years, long before I was born. Then it dawned on me. We as human beings are FAR more temporary than any of these inanimate objects and antiques. My house will probably outlive me; my antiques passed on or sold to another generation, quilts used by someone else, and maybe some of my items will end up in a museum, like old Viking helmets or wooden plows of the pioneer days. It is *we* as individual human beings who are temporarily here on this earth, not our things. Our things, our works, our legacy will outlive us, and we will be reflected only by what we leave behind, nothing more. Our spirit will be sent to God, our works, left behind on the earth.

Perhaps, we need to think more about what we are leaving behind, what we SHOULD leave behind, for the others that are following us. We will be gone and they will come. What do you want to pass on to the others? For me, I think I will pass on these things, hopefully. I want to pass on my appreciation for old things, my love of the earth, my faith in God, and, my love for my son, who hopefully will be filled with this love, and pass it on to his kids, and his kids to their kids, and on and on and on. Pass it on I say. Because someday, we will be gone, and love, after all, should be our greatest legacy.

Farewell

I have little treasure
To leave behind
Except these reflections
Of my heart's mind
Take what I have
And know that we are
Just here in passing
To the next star.